Picture-Perfect Mazes

Conceptis Puzzles

Sterling Publishing Co., Inc.
New York

To find out more about Conceptis Puzzles,
visit www.conceptispuzzles.com.

10 9 8 7 6 5 4 3 2 1

Published by Sterling Publishing Co., Inc.
387 Park Avenue South, New York, NY 10016
©2006 by Conceptis Puzzles
Distributed in Canada by Sterling Publishing
c/o Canadian Manda Group, 165 Dufferin Street
Toronto, Ontario, Canada M6K 3H6
Distributed in the United Kingdom by GMC Distribution Services
Castle Place, 166 High Street, Lewes, East Sussex, England BN7 1XU
Distributed in Australia by Capricorn Link (Australia) Pty. Ltd.
P.O. Box 704, Windsor, NSW 2756, Australia

Sterling ISBN-13: 978-1-4027-3868-5
ISBN-10: 1-4027-3868-4

For information about custom editions, special sales, premium and
corporate purchases, please contact Sterling Special Sales
Department at 800-805-5489 or specialsales@sterlingpub.com.

Contents

Introduction

Solve a maze and create a picture! There are two types of picture maze puzzles in this book, basic and reversed. To start out, solve each of these fun puzzles just as you would a traditional maze: find the true path by starting at the maze's entrance and drawing a line to the maze's exit, avoiding false paths and dead ends.

But the fun is not over once you exit! What's next? In the basic kind of maze, you color in the path you traced with a dark, thick line of pen or marker to create a picture. In the other kind, which we call the reversed maze (labeled R), after you have traced the true path lightly in pencil, color in all the wrong paths with a thick pen or pencil to create your picture.

You might be surprised to learn that picture mazes of this kind were invented in Japan over 20 years ago. Today picture mazes have a dedicated following among children and adults all over the world. By reversing the tones of the maze paths, we have been able to offer you more detailed pictures than were available with basic picture mazes alone, as well as recognizable portrait mazes. So grab your marker and pencil and get started!

Maze #1

Maze #2

Solutions on page 79

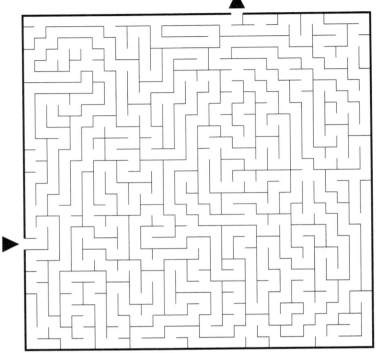

Solution on page 79

Maze #4

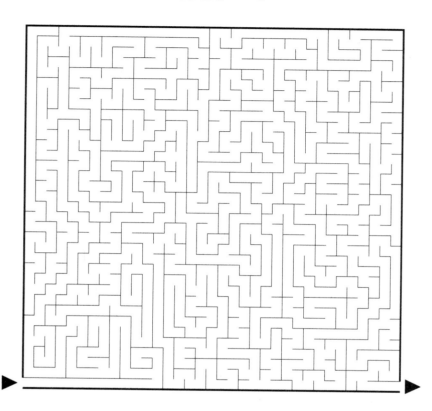

Solution on page 79

Maze #5

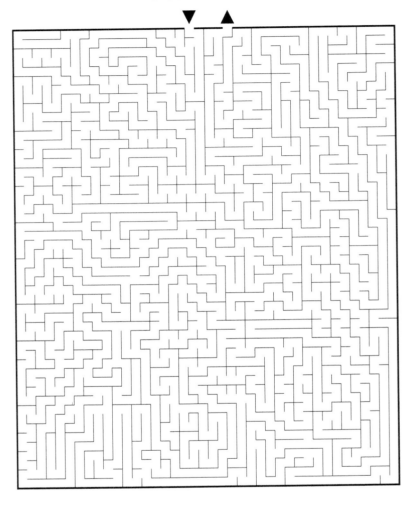

Solution on page 79

Maze #6

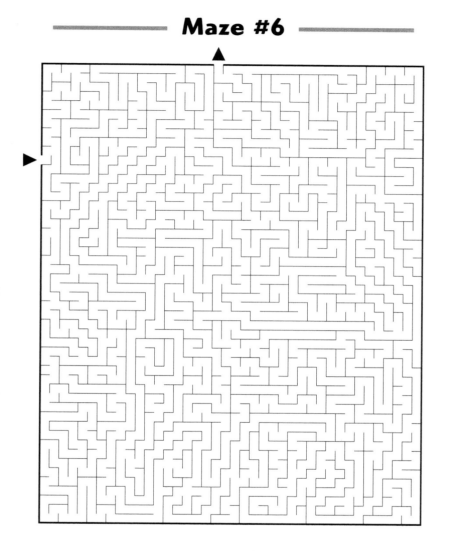

Solution on page 80

Maze #7

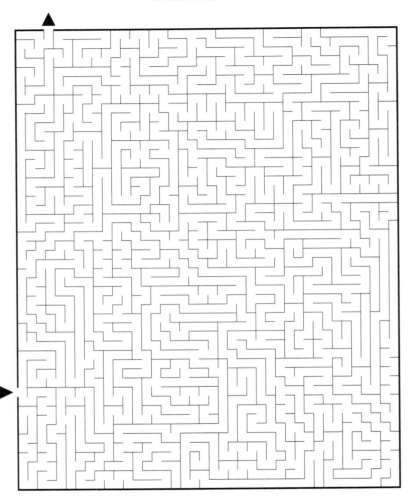

Solution on page 80

Maze #8

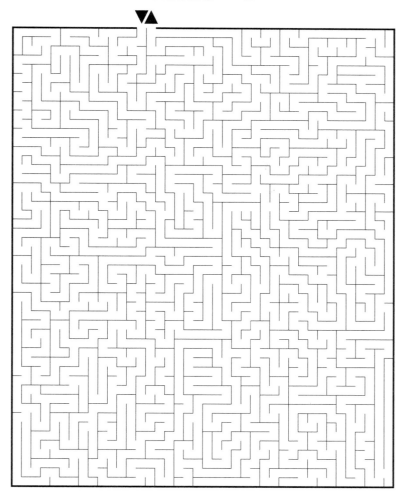

Solution on page 80

Maze #9

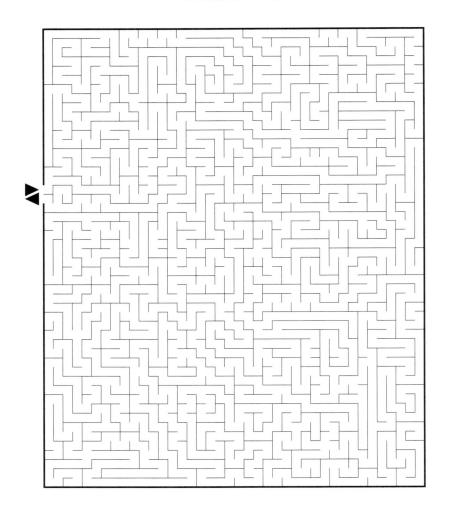

Solution on page 80

Maze #10

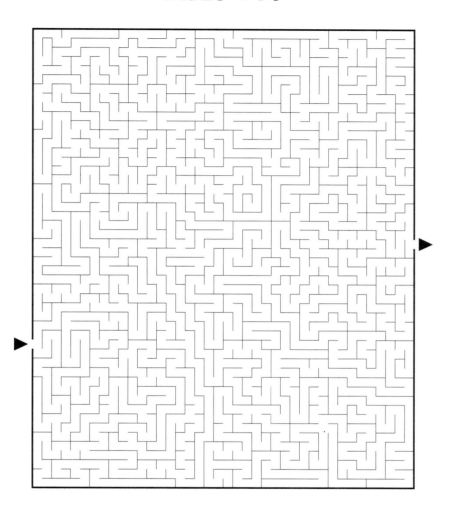

Solution on page 81

Maze #11

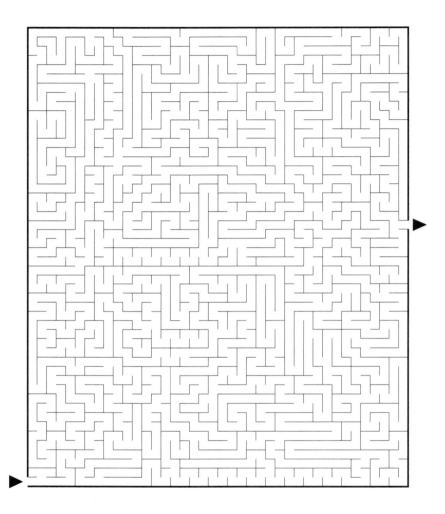

Solution on page 81

Maze #12

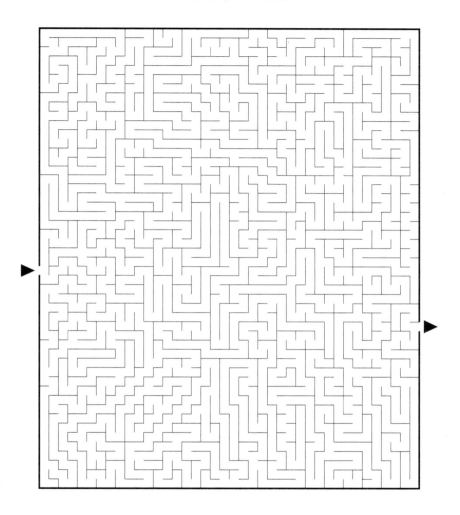

Solution on page 81

Maze #13

Solution on page 81

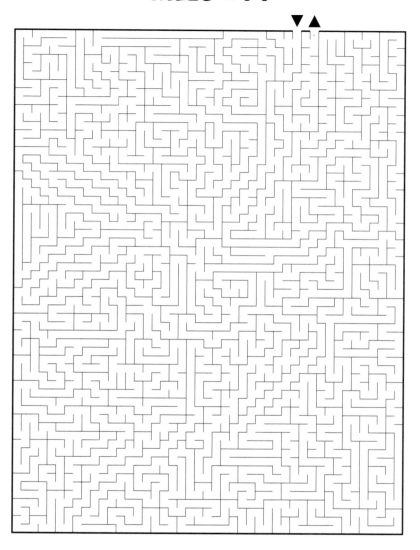

Solution on page 82

Maze #15

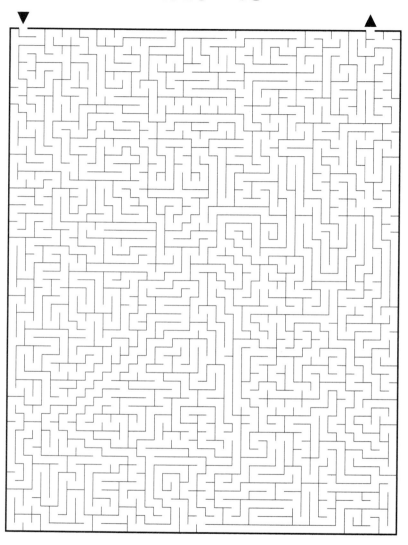

Solution on page 82

Maze #16

Solution on page 82

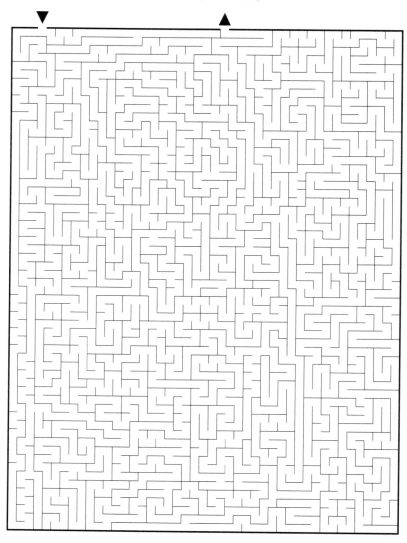

Solution on page 82

Maze #18

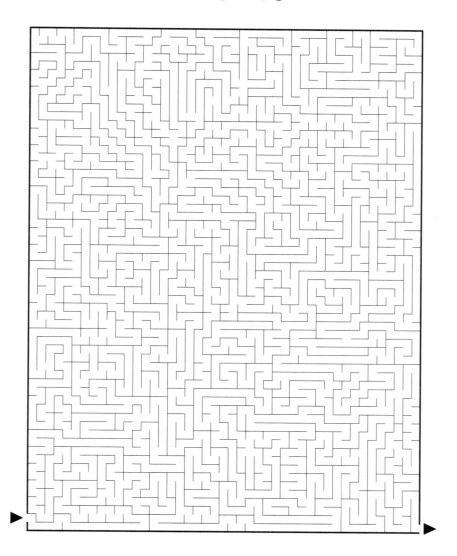

Solution on page 83

Maze #19

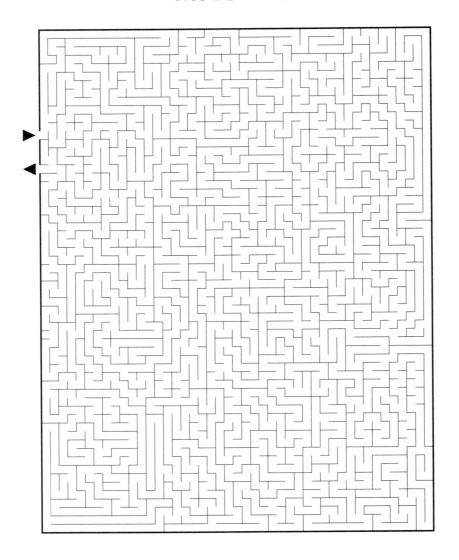

Solution on page 83

Maze #20

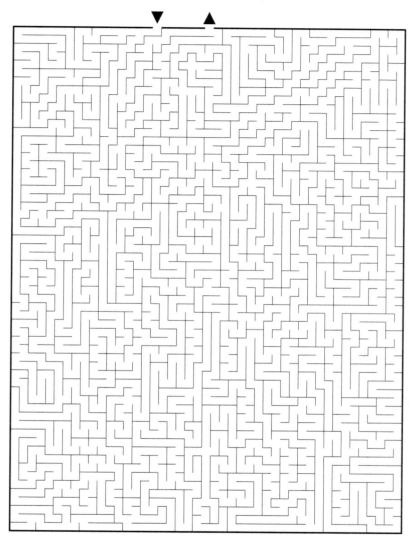

Solution on page 83

Maze #21

Maze #22

Solutions on page 83

Solution on page 84

Solution on page 84

Solution on page 84

Solution on page 84

Solution on page 84

Solution on page 85

Solution on page 85

Solution on page 85

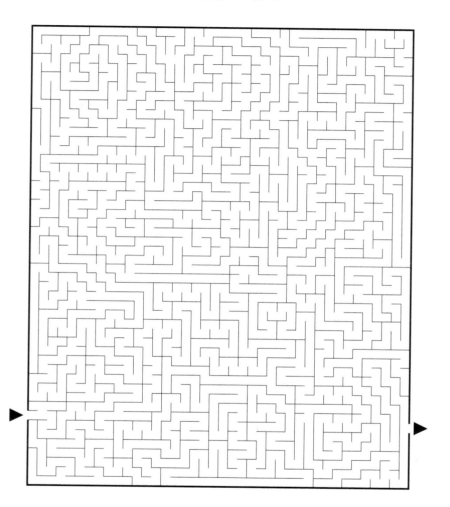

Solution on page 85

Maze #32

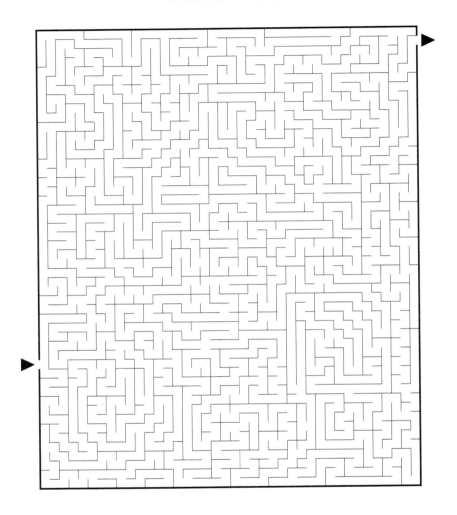

Solution on page 86

Maze #33

Solution on page 86

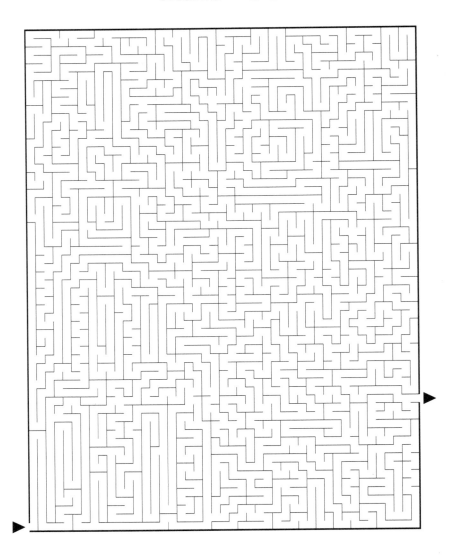

Solution on page 86

Maze #35

Solution on page 86

Solution on page 87

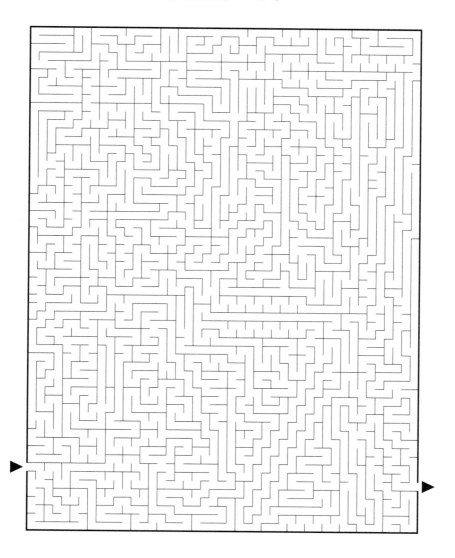

Solution on page 87

Maze #38

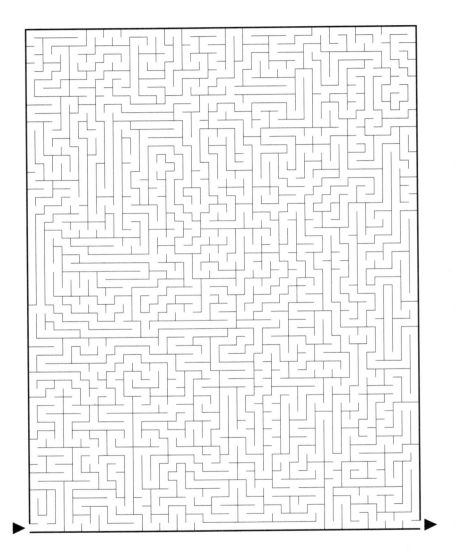

Solution on page 87

Maze #39

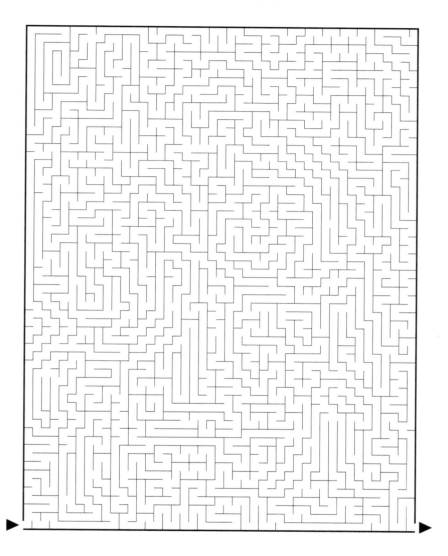

Solution on page 87

Maze #40

Maze #41

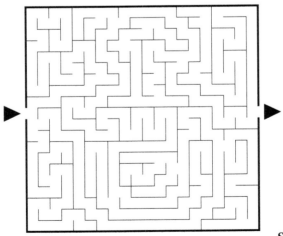

Solutions on page 88

Maze #42

Solution on page 88

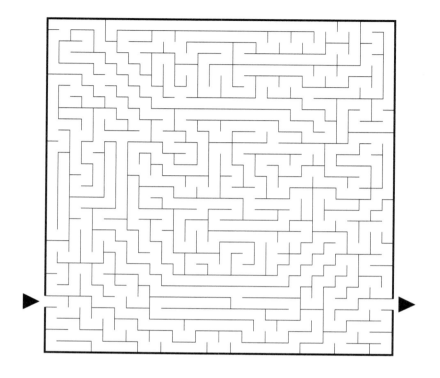

Solution on page 88

Maze #44

Solution on page 88

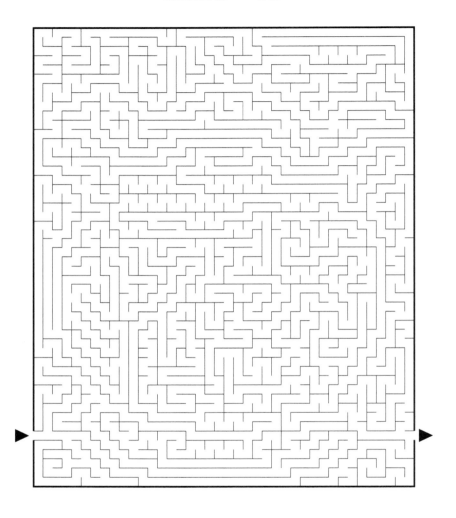

Solution on page 88

Maze #46

Solution on page 89

Solution on page 89

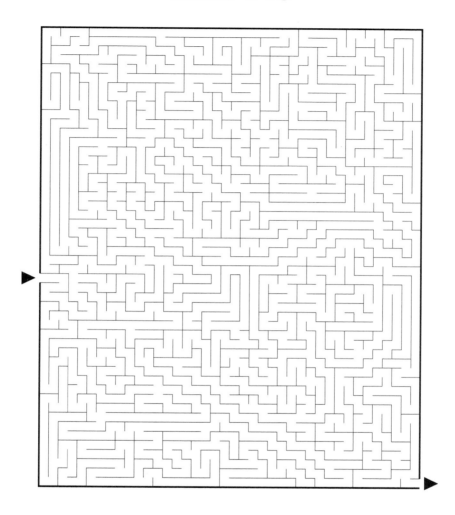

Solution on page 89

Maze #49

Solution on page 89

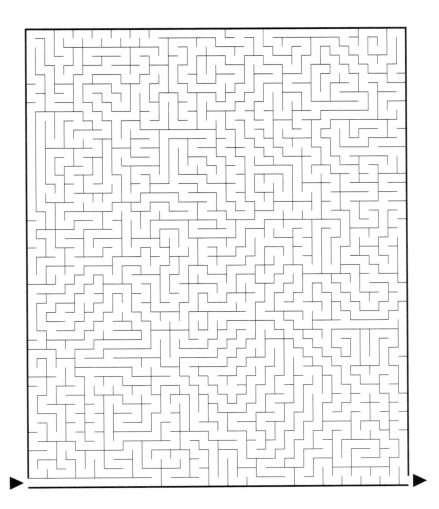

Solution on page 90

Maze #51

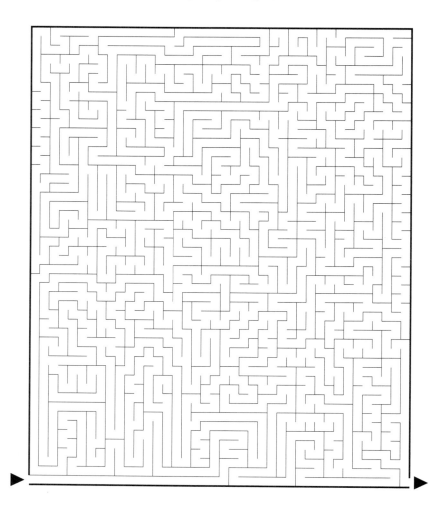

Solution on page 90

Maze #52

Solution on page 90

Solution on page 90

Solution on page 91

Solution on page 91

Solution on page 91

Solution on page 91

Solution on page 92

Solution on page 92

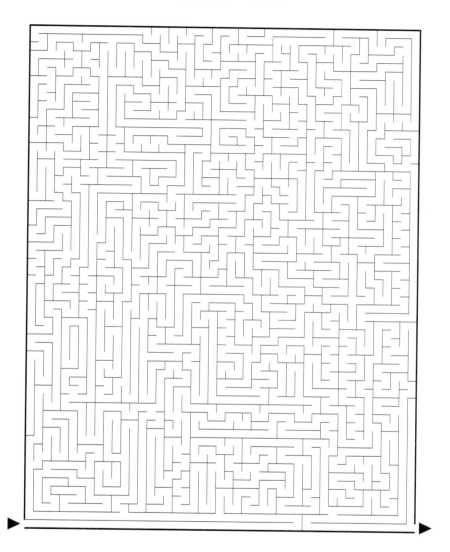

Solution on page 92

Maze #61

Solution on page 92

Solution on page 93

Solution on page 93

Solution on page 93

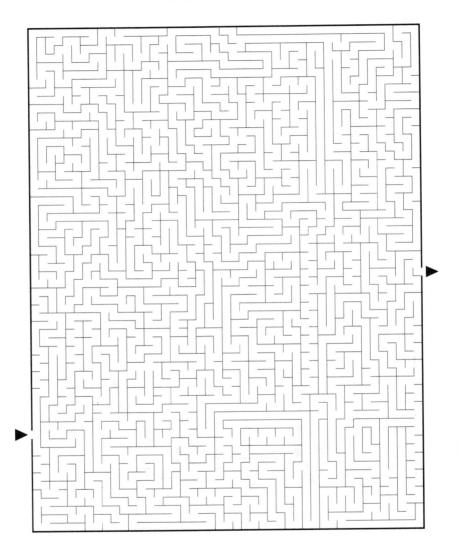

Solution on page 93

Maze #66

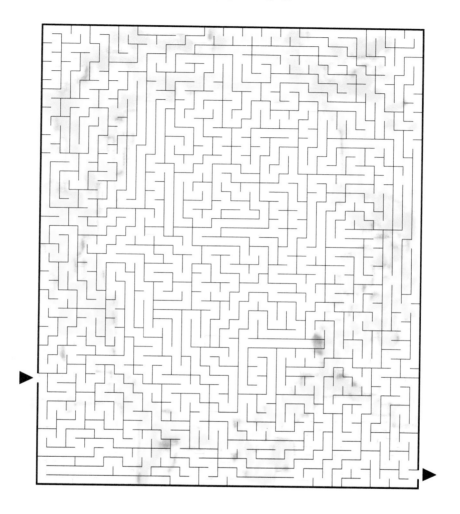

Solution on page 94

R This is a reversed maze. After you have traced the true path (solution) lightly in pencil, color in all the wrong paths with a thick pen or pencil to create your picture.

Solution on page 94

R This is a reversed maze. After you have traced the true path (solution) lightly in pencil, color in all the wrong paths with a thick pen or pencil to create your picture.

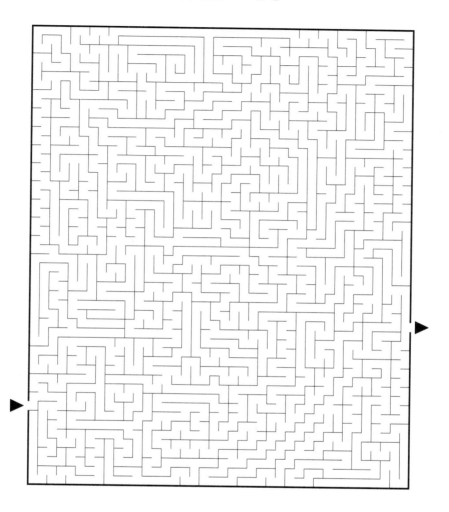

Solution on page 94

R This is a reversed maze. After you have traced the true path (solution) lightly in pencil, color in all the wrong paths with a thick pen or pencil to create your picture.

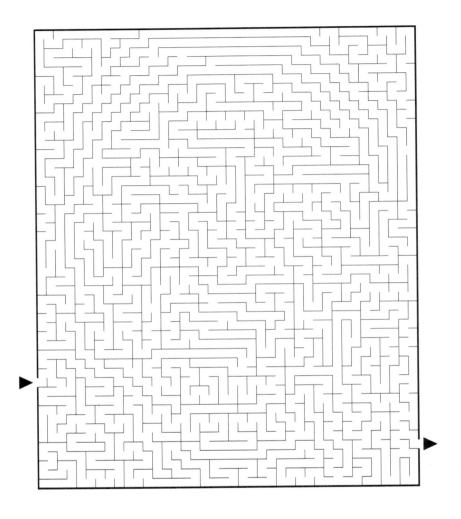

Solution on page 94

R This is a reversed maze. After you have traced the true path (solution) lightly in pencil, color in all the wrong paths with a thick pen or pencil to create your picture.

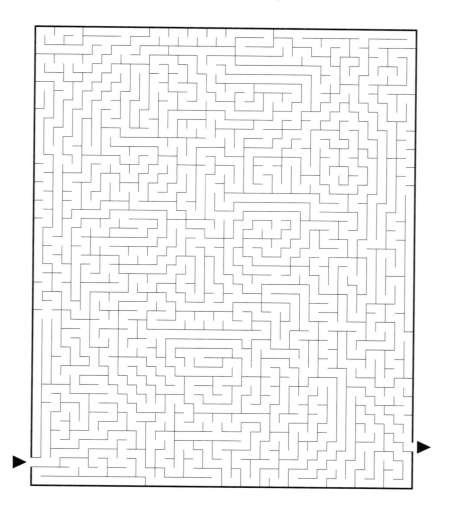

Solution on page 95

R This is a reversed maze. After you have traced the true path (solution) lightly in pencil, color in all the wrong paths with a thick pen or pencil to create your picture.

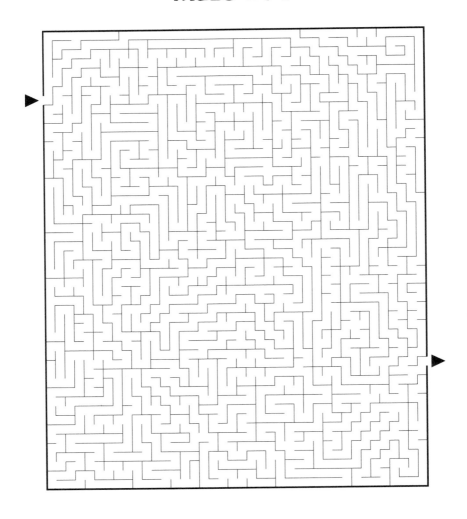

Solution on page 95

R This is a reversed maze. After you have traced the true path (solution) lightly in pencil, color in all the wrong paths with a thick pen or pencil to create your picture.

Maze #72

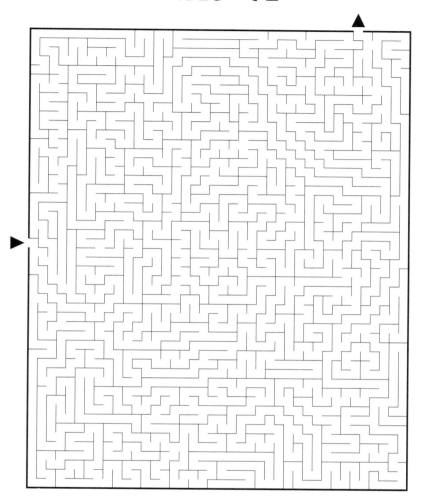

Solution on page 95

R This is a reversed maze. After you have traced the true
path (solution) lightly in pencil, color in all the wrong
paths with a thick pen or pencil to create your picture.

Maze #73

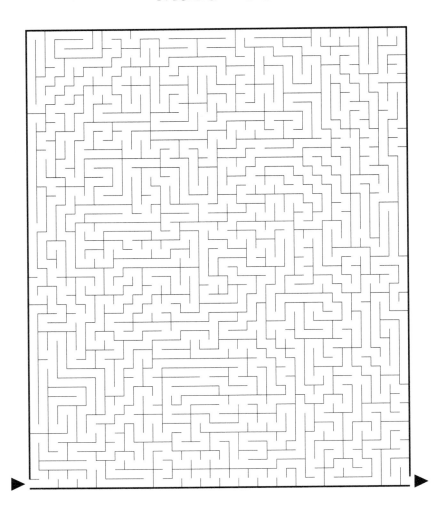

Solution on page 95

R This is a reversed maze. After you have traced the true path (solution) lightly in pencil, color in all the wrong paths with a thick pen or pencil to create your picture.

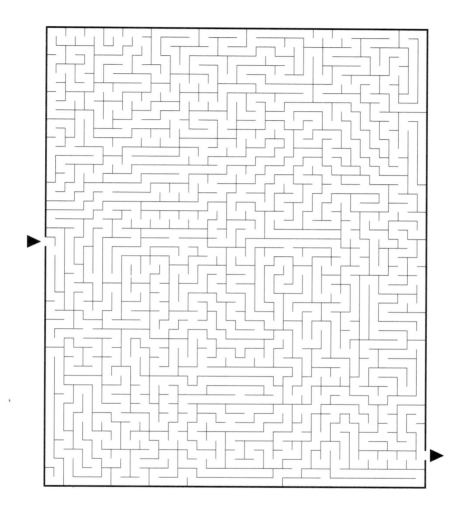

Solution on page 96

R This is a reversed maze. After you have traced the true path (solution) lightly in pencil, color in all the wrong paths with a thick pen or pencil to create your picture.

Maze #75

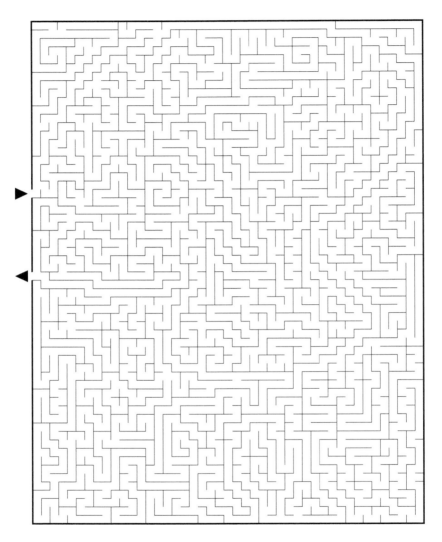

Solution on page 96

R This is a reversed maze. After you have traced the true path (solution) lightly in pencil, color in all the wrong paths with a thick pen or pencil to create your picture.

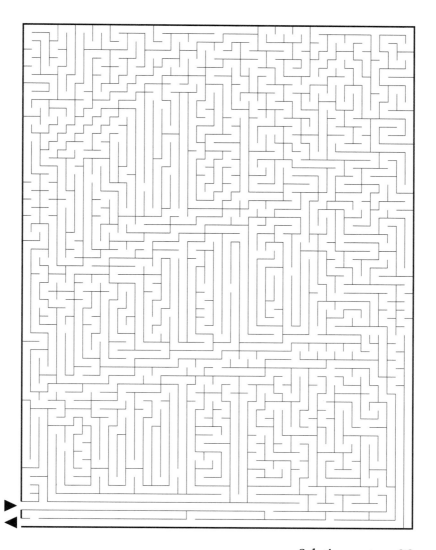

Solution on page 96

R This is a reversed maze. After you have traced the true path (solution) lightly in pencil, color in all the wrong paths with a thick pen or pencil to create your picture.

Maze #77

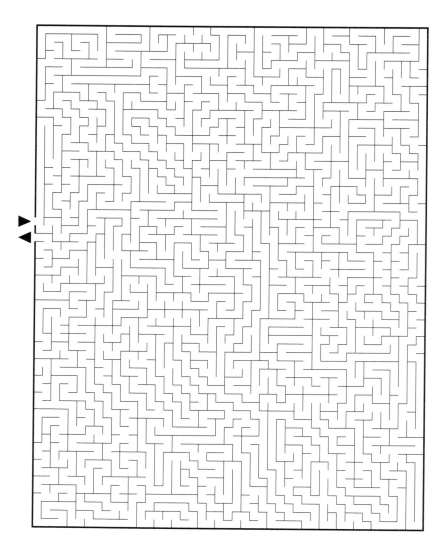

Solution on page 96

R This is a reversed maze. After you have traced the true path (solution) lightly in pencil, color in all the wrong paths with a thick pen or pencil to create your picture.

Solutions

Maze on page 7

Maze on page 5

Maze on page 5

Maze on page 8

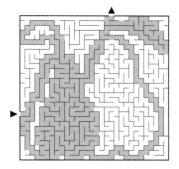

Maze on page 6

Solutions

Maze on page 9

Maze on page 11

Maze on page 10

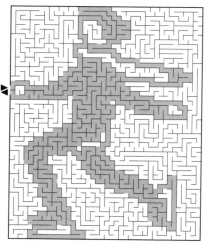

Maze on page 12

Solutions

Maze on page 15

Maze on page 13

Maze on page 16

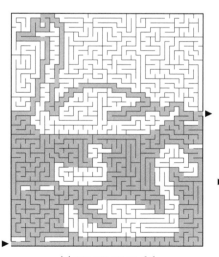

Maze on page 14

Solutions

Maze on page 17

Maze on page 19

Maze on page 18

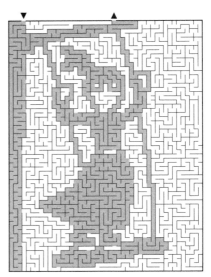

Maze on page 20

Solutions

Maze on page 21

Maze on page 23

Maze on page 24

Maze on page 22

Maze on page 24

Solutions

Maze on page 25

Maze on page 26

Maze on page 28

Maze on page 27

Maze on page 29

Solutions

Maze on page 32

Maze on page 30

Maze on page 31

Maze on page 33

Solutions

Maze on page 34

Maze on page 36

Maze on page 35

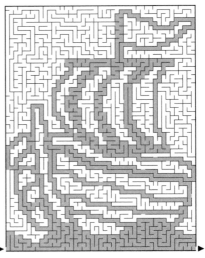

Maze on page 37

Solutions

Maze on page 38

Maze on page 40

Maze on page 39

Maze on page 41

Solutions

Maze on page 42

Maze on page 42

Maze on page 45

Maze on page 43

Maze on page 44

Maze on page 46

Solutions

Maze on page 49

Maze on page 47

Maze on page 50

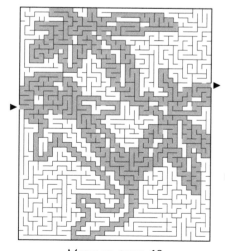

Maze on page 48

Solutions

Maze on page 51

Maze on page 53

Maze on page 52

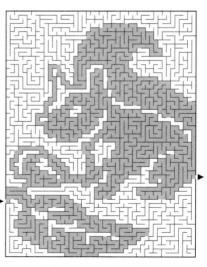

Maze on page 54

Solutions

Maze on page 57

Maze on page 55

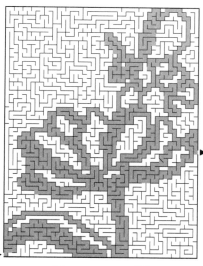

Maze on page 58

Maze on page 56

Solutions

Maze on page 59

Maze on page 61

Maze on page 60

Maze on page 62

Solutions

Maze on page 63

Maze on page 65

Maze on page 64

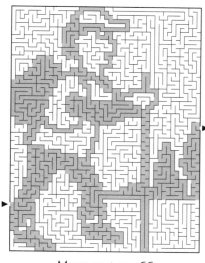

Maze on page 66

Solutions

Maze on page 67

Maze on page 69

Maze on page 68

Maze on page 70

Solutions

Maze on page 73

Maze on page 71

Maze on page 74

Maze on page 72

Solutions

Maze on page 75

Maze on page 77

Maze on page 76

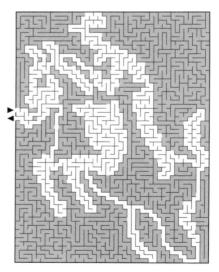

Maze on page 78